Robinson-Tabb House

A Chapter of Berkeley County History

Dave McMillion

International Standard Book Number 0-87012-887-6
Printed in the United States of America
Copyright © 2018 by Dave McMillion
Martinsburg, WV
All Rights Reserved
2018

McClain Printing Company
Parsons, WV
www.mcclainprinting.com
2018

Preface

My first wife, Vivian, came to me one day and told me what she had found: an old two-story brick Federal-style farmhouse off Welltown Road just north of Martinsburg, W.Va.

I was immediately hooked.

Though I never worked as a farmer, I grew up around them during my summer weekends as a kid at my great-grandfather's home in Greenbrier County.

What was not to like there? It was unspoiled beauty in rolling farmland. The smell of fresh summer mornings in southern West Virginia was made all the more mystical by fog slowly lifting off the Greenbrier River valley.

And the farmers? They rocked. My friend Milton Renick rolling past in his Ford pickup truck covered with mud and straw hanging out the tailgate told me this had to be my future somehow.

I never made it to farming. I ended up at West Virginia University where I learned to be a news reporter.

But when I saw the Robinson-Tabb House, it gave me a chance to live this life somehow.

What struck me about the place was the authenticity of it: as if the hay balers had just been put away in the barns the night before.

Old wooden crates in one of the barns still had the remains of farm-raised potatoes in them. A few pieces of equipment were still scattered in a bank barn, and I found any number of rusted, curious-looking implements in a rubbish heap.

Vivian and I started working on the place, tearing down through existing floors trying to find the original ones. We spent endless days painting, landscaping and tackling carpentry details. Our friend André Frye took care of the complicated tasks related to drywall work, cabinetry, wiring and plumbing.

Vivian's dreams - which included running Alexander Robinson's Antiques out of an adjacent stone cottage - were on a brief course. She died of cancer in 2004.

I lived at the house alone a while, entertaining myself playing guitar while continuing necessary duties.

i

One day, after my vocal teacher said I needed to sing in front of people at a bar if I really wanted to learn how perform, I met my second wife, Gail Mays.

There she stood, across from me in the back room at Shepherdstown's Mecklenburg Inn, while I frantically thought about which Grateful Dead songs to sing.

We married and have continued on at the Robinson-Tabb House while maintaining our Shepherdstown home.

Life moves on and we are ready to part with the Robinson-Tabb House to follow our lives and let someone else enjoy the old place.

The Robinson-Tabb House is no more spectacular than thousands of other beautiful historic homes across the Mountain State. But it has its own heart-warming stories, ones that should not be lost as the Eastern Panhandle continues to grow.

Like the Dillon Farm Museum over the hill from the property, the house should stand as a monument to Berkeley County's early settlement days and allow people to learn about Berkeley County's agricultural past.

A special thank you goes to members of the Riner family, the last farming family at the property, for taking time with me to conduct oral interviews about the history of the farm.

I also want to thank John Frye at the John Clinton Frye Western Maryland Room of the Washington County Free Library in Hagerstown, Md., the Martinsburg-Berkeley County Public Library, and the Berkeley County Historical Society for their research help. The Berkeley County Historical Society also worked to get the house listed on the National Register of Historic Places in 2004.

I appreciate last-minute help from my newspaper colleague Andy Schotz regarding editorial advice.

And a special thanks also goes to the West Virginia Division of Culture and History for a grant for slate roof repair and helping us stay on track with the best preservation techniques. Thanks to the state, these partnerships are possible to keep the history of the great Mountain State alive. Contractors and local businesses also helped make all this possible, including V.E. Mauck Plumbing Supplies in Martinsburg, S.G. Plumbing in Kearneysville, Heritage Roofing in Martinsburg, Ellsworth Electric in Hagerstown, Above Board Contracting, Berkeley Glass, Cumberland Valley Heating and Air Conditioning, Master Masonry and McClain Printing Co., in Parsons, W.Va., for printing this book.

- Dave McMillion

Chapter 1

Putting Down Roots

Vast sections of land in Berkeley County in the 1700s were owned by Lord Fairfax of England. In 1767, a large section of land on Welltown Road was granted to Robert Paul from Lord Fairfax. After Paul died, his heirs conveyed the acreage to a relative who sold one half of the property to Alexander Robinson. Robinson acquired the other half of the property in 1810.

According to the Berkeley County Historical Society, the Robinsons were a wealthy family which owned various mills in the county.

As was common at the time, Robinson turned to natural resources for shelter, constructing his 1 1/2 story home from logs.

In keeping with a tradition, the front door was faced to the south away from northern winds and to take advantage of the warming rays of the sun in the winter.

Old timbers can still be seen under the log section that is now the kitchen. Parts of the log section can also be seen in the attic above the kitchen. When the house was rewired after 1999 and plaster was stripped away for wiring, the log structure could be seen extending through the wall dividing the central staircase from the living room and parlor.

According to West Virginia Division of Culture and History records, Robinson built his log home in 1818, shortly before his death.

George W. Tabb Jr., a member of a pioneer family who migrated from the Tidewater area of Virginia before the Revolutionary War, acquired the property in 1828, according to the records.

About 1839, Tabb started construction on the brick section of the house that can be seen today.

Walking through the Robinson-Tabb House is like walking through a different era, conveyed through features like two large pocket doors dividing the living room from a parlor area. The doors feature a unique grain-painted design with white porcelain knobs.

A walk up the center staircase is a treat on a warm day when the reward at the end is walking onto the second-floor porch for a view of the property and rolling Berkeley County farmland in the distance.

"It's a great house," said David L. Taylor, a historic preservation specialist who completed research work to place the house on the National Register of Historic Places.

Taylor, who served as executive director of the Columbus Landmarks Foundation and chaired the Pennsylvania State Historic Preservation Board, said the wood ceiling in the dining room is typical of log architecture. The house was built using pre-industrial skills, meaning that wood in the house was hand-planed, according to Taylor.

The brick section is federal style, which was the first national style in America after the Revolution, according to Taylor. It was influenced by English designs.

The farm, which once spread across what is the Harlan Run subdivision today, also included a cluster of farm buildings,

2

including a massive bank barn. Across from the house is a stone cottage which dates to the same period of the house, although the construction date is not known, according to state records.

According to the Riners, the last farming family in the house, there is a root cellar on the hillside facing Holden Drive. It was filled in.

Paul Riner, one of nine children in the Riner family, said a kiln was used at the site to fire bricks for the brick addition.

At one time, it was common for brick masons to fire bricks on site, according to brickarchitecture.com.

The skill of brick construction crossed the Atlantic Ocean with Dutch and British immigrants, some of whom were brick masons, according to the website.

Undated aerial photo of the farm.

Chapter 2

The Tabbs, Slavery and Growth of Berkeley County

The Robinson-Tabb House reflects the growth of Berkeley County from its time of settlement "when the most rudimentary shelter served the needs of those clearing the land," according to West Virginia Division of Culture and History records.

Berkeley County originally took in all of Jefferson County and two-thirds of Morgan County, according to wvencyclopedia.org.

The county was cut out of Frederick County Va., in 1772 and was named in honor of Norborne Berkeley, a colonial governor of Virginia, according to the website.

The first known Tabb in the United States was Humphrey Tabb from Wiltshire, England, according to a paper presented by Dorthea Feigley during a 1973 meeting of the Berkeley County Historical Society.

The Tabbs went on to create a substantial part of the region's history.

Humphrey Tabb owned land at the mouth of the Potomac River at the Chesapeake Bay in 1637 in Elizabeth County, according to Feigley, who spoke on "Tabb Land Past and Present."

Humphrey Tabb's line can be traced to four Tabb brothers in Berkeley County: Robert, William, George and Edward, according to Feigley.

Robert, William and George were in the American Revolution and participated in the Beeline March to Boston, according to Feigley.

Robert Tabb was killed in 1775 and George Washington gave William and George honorable discharges so they could settle their brother's estate, Feigley said.

Edward Tabb built "Rural Hill" another National Register of Historic Places home which is just up the hill from the Robinson-Tabb House off Ridge Road.

Feigley's paper mentions George W. Tabb Jr., and his work to expand the Robinson-Tabb House.

Feigley said the value of the land while Tabb owned it jumped in 1840 and in 1844, suggesting this is when he made his expansions to the house.

Tabb was identified as a farmer in census records and owned the property until 1866, according to state records. Three years before his death in 1869, Tabb turned over his 205 acres to Cromwell Riner Sperow, according to state division of culture and history records.

The Sperows had the farm until 1948, when it was turned over to James A. Riner, whose family owned the tract until 1999 when it was sold for the Harlan Run subdivision.

The Robinson-Tabb House stood as the western portion of Virginia was divided to create West Virginia in 1863.

In 1872, a constitution was drafted for the state, meaning officials in the new state had to set up machinery for their government.

In 1891, the state created the State Board of Agriculture, and Gov. A.B. Fleming appointed Cromwell Sperow as one of the first members of the board, according to the book "History of Berkeley County West Virginia" by Willis F. Evans.

The Robinson-Tabb House also has ties to the nation's slavery era.

The Robinsons and the Tabbs were slave owners and it is believed the stone cottage may have been used for slave quarters.

Berkeley County was a slave-owning region with some plantations having 100 or more enslaved persons, according to wvencyclopedia.org.

In 1830, two years after Tabb acquired the farm, the census listed 1,034 male slaves and 885 female slaves in the county, according to the website. There were 276 free blacks, it said.

Tabb's connection to slavery is illustrated by an advertisement placed in the Martinsburg Gazette in 1834 in which Tabb offered "servants" for hire.

The ad read: "The following servants; a woman with two children, one about six the other two years of age; she is a good cook and washer. Also, a boy and girl, the boy seventeen or eighteen, the girl fifteen or sixteen years of age, with a smaller boy and girl, the boy large enough to go errands, and the girl to nurse."

According to Cora Mae Stuckey, one of the Riner children, a black midwife named Annie Holly handled deliveries at the Robinson-Tabb House. The Riners carried on a tradition of large farming families in the region with nine children. Stuckey said six were born in the house.

According to Stuckey, Holly lived in Nipetown, a community just north of Martinsburg. Holly claimed her ancestors were slaves at the Robinson-Tabb House, according to Stuckey.

Daisy Ellwood, Stuckey's aunt, remembered Holly's time at the farm, like her propensity of smoking a pipe.

"She moved from one place to another," Ellwood said.

Holly was the daughter of Lena Brown, a Nipetown resident whose grandfather, William Phenex, built a "colored school" in Hedgesville, according to the book, "Architectural and Pictorial History of Berkeley County," published by the Berkeley County Historical Society.

The original Lena Brown House burned, according to the book.

Chapter 3

Life at the Farm

The Robinson-Tabb House stood witness to the Civil War, when the nation was sharply divided between the north and the south. It was there during the 1918 flu pandemic and witnessed the sweat and determination of those who made it through the Great Depression of the 1930s as they sharecropped land to put food on the table.

It created lasting memories of farming by the moonlight, found and lost love, big families, teamwork and traditions.

Before Riner acquired the farm, he sharecropped the land in the midst of the Depression in the 1930s, according to Stuckey. Sharecropping was a system of agriculture in which a landowner allows a tenant to use the land in return for a share of the crops.

Riner raised corn, wheat and barley and ran a dairy until his death on Dec. 14, 1980.

Stuckey and her husband Floyd stopped by the house one day to talk about their memories on the farm.

Floyd recalled how the front sunroom off the kitchen used to be an open porch. There was a bench on the porch, and when the farm workers came in from the fields, they used a bucket of water to wash off with before meals.

"Homemade bread was made in this house almost every day," Cora Mae said.

Stuckey said the family didn't have electric until the 1950s.

"I remember the kerosene lights," said Cora Mae, recalling an Aladdin model which hung from the ceiling in the dining room.

Whether it was the crops which were grown there or the animals which were raised, nothing went to waste.

Even time was a precious commodity.

After the cows were milked in the evening, Cora Mae said she remembers going into the fields at harvest time.

"We used to get the old horses hooked-up and go out and pick up corn in the moonlight," she said.

Milking was handled in the mornings and evenings, and Cora Mae said she remembered heading to the barn in the evenings with a lantern.

Riner branched-out into other areas, selling his potatoes and raising sheep and hogs, which handed him a new revenue source: his own country hams.

Hogs were raised in a building not far from the kitchen, and when it came time for butchering, about eight of them were loaded onto a wagon and shot, said Harold Johns, Riner's son-in-law.

The wagon was pulled down to a rectangular-shaped barn that today is attached to the cottage.

A hog-slaughtering system was set up in the building, which included a rail in the ceiling where the hogs were hung.

There were different stages in the process as the hogs were moved down the rail like an assembly line.

Johns said he helped on the farm, and recalled preparations for the slaughtering.

"The next morning as soon as they got the milking done, there would be a pile of us that had a job to do," Johns said.

The carcasses were scalded so hair could be removed, and other men in the butchering party had chores, such as bringing in wood and firing up kettles that were used to make products like pon haus, which is a mush of pork scraps and trimmings combined with cornmeal and flour.

"Mr. Riner didn't waste nothing. He went down to the feet of a hog," Johns said.

Hogs were slid along a curve in the rail, which extended into another room behind the cottage. A giant concrete sink of sorts was constructed in the room, allowing workers to rinse entrails into a septic system which is still in place.

Riner's country hams were made with a seasoning recipe that was handed-down over the generations, Floyd Stuckey said.

"City people, once they got a country ham from him, they wouldn't want to buy it from anybody else," said Cora Mae.

Riner hung his hams in a smokehouse. "I'd seen that old smokehouse so full you couldn't get one between another," Floyd Stuckey said.

Charles R. Beall said he remembered his father, C. Ralph Beall, doing legal work for Riner, who would compensate Beall with apples and hams.

Beall said he can remember getting Christmas hams from the farm in tough economic times in the 1940s.

"I just remember so many children," Beall said.

Christmas time meant large gatherings.

Paul Riner said his family always gathered in the living room, and considering he had eight siblings, that made for big crowds.

"You take nine kids, and all their kids, that's quite a few," he said.

Love found at the farm included a story of three brothers and three sisters.

While Jim Riner married his wife Nellie, Nellie's sister Bessie married Jim's brother Howard, and Jim's other brother Marvin married Nellie's other sister Daisy, who lived until she was 100.

Paul Riner said he remembers himself and other boys in the family sleeping in the back bedroom, which meant some interesting times in winter.

Because windows in the room had cracks in them, Paul said he remembered times when snow would blow through.

"We were boys, just young boys, sleeping in a big old feather tick," he said.

Paul recounted other memories, like playing with black snakes in a cedar tree and watering horses at the farm's hand-dug well. The well has been a consistent source of water, once providing water to the barn complex as well as the house.

Today, it is under a concrete floor in a small room attached to the cottage.

"I have seen down in that. When we were kids, the building wasn't there and there were just boards over that well," Paul said.

Two cisterns also still exist, one being just outside the main door to the cottage and the other under the floor of the sunroom in the house.

Although many old ways of farm life are fading from memory, some people in the county are working to prevent it.

It's ironic that the Robinson-Tabb House would end up just over the hill from an organization that works to preserve the county's agricultural traditions.

The Dillon Farm Museum at the intersection of Ridge Road and Hedgesville Road offers the public an extensive collection of antique farm equipment, including a threshing machine that was donated by the Riner family.

A threshing machine was an implement that "threshed" or separated seeds of a plant from the stalks and husks. The process involved beating the plant to cause grains to fall out.

Paul Riner said his father bought the threshing machine in 1936. Paul said he always remembered the date because it was the year Cora Mae was born. Paul said his dad owned the threshing machine until his death, at which time it was left to his wife.

No one used the threshing machine anymore and when the museum was starting, the family decided to donate it for the museum, Paul Riner said.

"It just made a home for the old threshing machine," he said.

The Dillon Farm Museum was formed after L. Norman Dillon, a retired farmer in the Apple Pie Ridge section of the county, became concerned about the disappearance of agricultural life in the Eastern Panhandle.

He set aside money to help with planning an agricultural museum, and the facility was dedicated in 1987.

The 8.3-acre site, once a part of the Dillon farm, pays tribute to the county's early agriculturalists and offers younger generations a chance to learn about the way of life, according to the organization's website.

The Riners were the last farming family in the home. James and Nellie Riner had nine children, six of whom were born in the house.

Chapter 4

Change and the Future
of the Robinson-Tabb House

Life is a cycle of change and it came again to the Robinson-Tabb House in 1999 when the farm, which extended from Welltown Road to Ridge Road, was sold to meet the housing needs of the growing Eastern Panhandle.

The development became known as Harlan Run, named for a stream that once meandered through the farm, according to Paul Riner.

Riner said the stream used to be a constant-flowing run until ponds used in other development were established next to a nearby mountain.

Today, the outline of the stream can still be seen in the development as it serves as an area to collect excess storm water during heavy precipitation.

Bridges were constructed over the stream bed as part of Harlan Run, giving a reminder of the creek that once entertained kids on summer days.

"When I was a kid, I could swim in it," Paul Riner recalled.

One road to the farm originally extended off Welltown Road and made a straight line to the house. After Harlan Run started, the road was removed and Holden Drive, the main entrance to the development, was created off Welltown Road.

Holden Drive now curves through the old farm, and after crossing one of the bridges just past Periwinkle Place, the Robinson-Tabb House sits in the distance, a steady reminder of the Robinsons, Tabbs, Sperows and Riners and the farm lives they led there.

The accompanying barns, including the cavernous bank barn in the middle of the complex, were dismantled to make way for Harlan Run.

It might strike a sad note for some, but it is impossible to save everything.

Sometimes, as George W. Tabb Jr.'s wife Elizabeth realized when she died at the house in 1847, God hands down a fate that is not always understood.

Elizabeth Tabb had been ill for five years and five months when she died at 54. According to her obituary, Elizabeth was "often heard to say - the Lord's will be done; and again, in other words - if it, was His will, she was willing to depart and go hence."

The Riners donated their threshing machine to the L. Norman Dillon Farm Museum near Hedgesville, W.Va.

A stone cottage near the house dates to the same period as the home. It may have been used for enslaved people during the farm's early days.

The Robinson-Tabb House was placed on the National Register of Historic Places on Feb. 11, 2004.

Among the home's unique features are large pocket doors in the living/parlor area.

The main entrance to the house.